How to Eat a Pizza

1 Cut   **2** Read   **3**

1
2
3
4

Bite into the pizza.

Lick your lips!

Pick up the biggest part.

Cut the pizza into parts.

How to Use the Telephone

1 Cut **2** Read **3** Paste in order

1	
2	
3	
4	

Talk to your friend.

Hang up the telephone.

Pick up the telephone.

Call the number you want.

How to Feed the Cat

1 Cut   **2** Read   **3** Paste in order

1

2

3

4

Take the lid off the can.

Call your cat.

Put the cat food in the dish.

Get a can of cat food and a dish.

How to Drink Milk

1 Cut   **2** Read   **3** Paste in order

1
2
3
4

Put the glass in the sink.

Get a glass. Then get out the cold milk.

Sit down and drink the milk.

Fill the glass to the top.

How to Work a Yo-Yo

1 Cut   **2** Read   **3** Paste in order

1
2
3
4

Do this again and again.

Wrap the string on to the yo-yo.

Drop the yo-yo, then pull it up.

Put the end of the string on your finger.

How to Make a Mask

1 Cut   **2** Read   **3** Paste in order

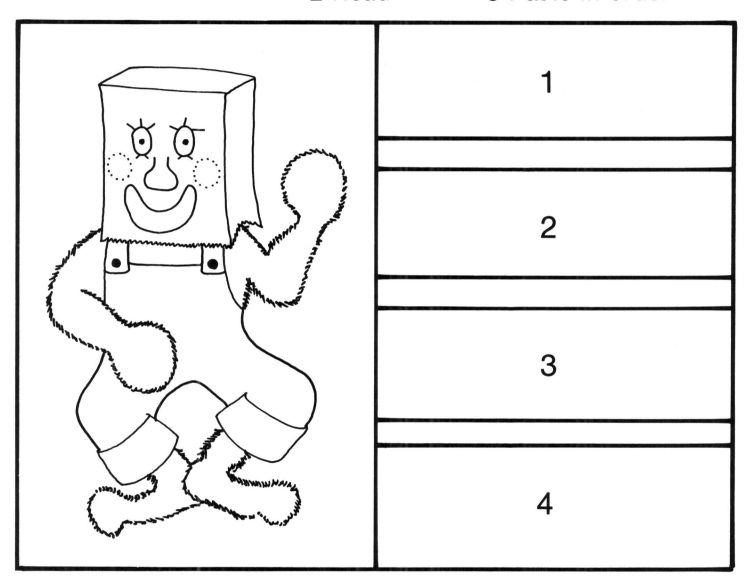

1

2

3

4

Put on the mask and surprise your pal.

Get a big brown bag.

Cut out two eyes so you can see.

Now draw a nose and a mouth.

How to Put on a Jacket

1 Cut   **2** Read   **3** Paste in order

1

2

3

4

Put your arms in the sleeves.

Zip up your jacket.

It is a cold day. Get your jacket.

Now you can go out to play.

How to Eat a Cookie

1 Cut   **2** Read   **3** Paste in order

	1
	2
	3
	4

Take big bites and eat them up.

Take your cookies outside and sit on the back step.

Lick the last bits off your fingers.

Take two cookies out of the box.

How to Ride a Bike

1 Cut   **2** Read   **3** Paste in order

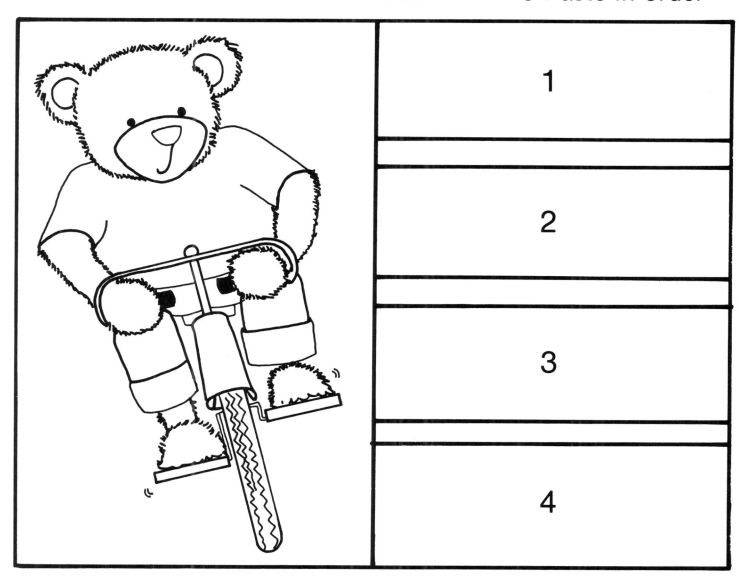

1

2

3

4

Push the pedals 🦶 so you can go down the street.

Put on the brakes to stop.

Get on the bike.

Put your feet on the pedals and your hands on the handlebars. 🦶

How to Make an Ice Cream Cone

1 Cut   **2** Read   **3** Paste in order

1	
2	
3	
4	

Take a big lick and gobble it down.

Then get the ice cream from the freezer.

First get a scoop and a cone.

Take a big scoop of ice cream and put it on the cone.

How to ___ ___ur Dog a Bath

1 Cut   ___ad   **3** Paste in order

	1
	2
	3
	4
	5
	6

Put him in the water.

Wash the suds off the dog.

Dry him with the big towel and let him go.

Now catch your dog.

Fill a tub with water and get a big towel.

Rub the suds all over your dog.

How to Paint a Fence

1 Cut   **2** Read   **3** Paste in order

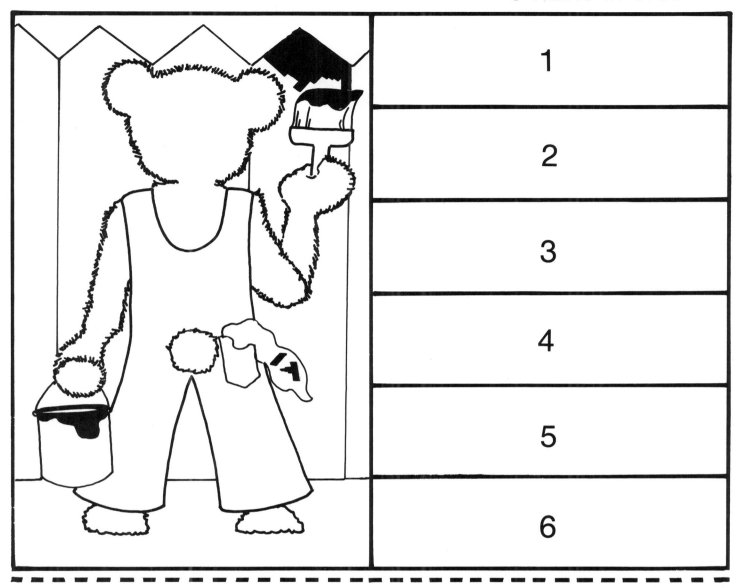

1
2
3
4
5
6

See if you missed some spots.

Now get a can of paint and a brush.

Dress in something old.

Clean the brush and put it away.

Wipe the dirt off the fence.

Brush the paint onto the fence.

Sequencing Short Stories   12

How to Catch a Tadpole

1 Cut   **2** Read   **3** Paste in order

1
2
3
4
5
6

Put holes in the lid.

Look in the water until you see tadpoles.

Put the lid on the jar and take them home.

Find a jar at your house.

Go to a pond.

Scoop up some tadpoles in your jar.

How to Pick an Apple

1 Cut   **2** Read   **3** Paste in order

1
2
3
4
5
6

Get a bag and a ladder.

Take the bag of apples into the house.

Pick the apples and put them in the bag.

Go down the ladder.

Go up the ladder.

Put the ladder by the tree.

Sequencing Short Stories 14

How to Wrap a Gift

1 Cut   **2** Read   **3** Paste in order

1
2
3
4
5
6

Wrap the box in pretty paper.

Set the gift in a box.

Now put on the lid.

Tape a ribbon on the box.

Stick a card under the ribbon.

Take the gift to the party.

How to Make Your Bed

1 Cut   **2** Read   **3** Paste in order

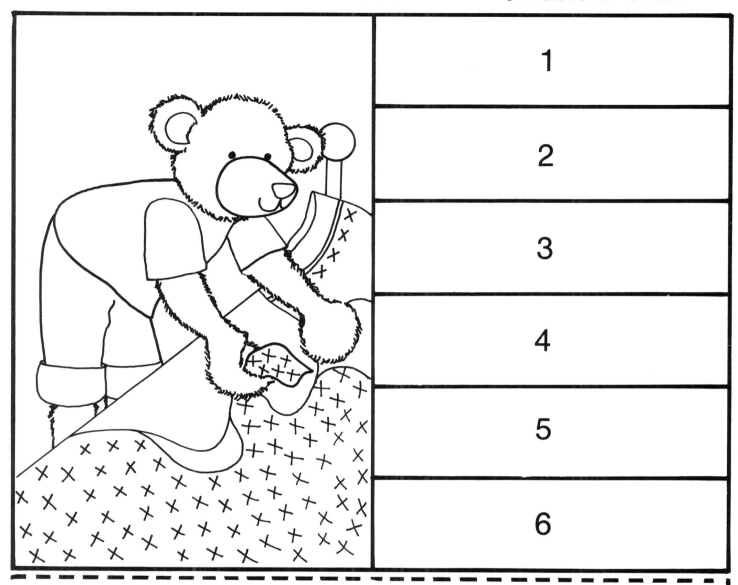

| 1 |
| 2 |
| 3 |
| 4 |
| 5 |
| 6 |

Fix the blanket.

Fluff the pillow and set it on the bed.

Put the bedspread on top.

Get out of bed.

Call your mom to see the good job you did.

Pull up the sheets.

How to Make a Jack-O'-Lantern

1 Cut   **2** Read   **3** Paste in order

1
2
3
4
5
6

Cut out eyes, nose, and a mouth.

Pick a big, orange pumpkin

Set it in the window.

Put a candle in the jack-o'-lantern.

Cut off the top.

Take out all of the seeds.

How to Take a Bath

1 Cut   **2** Read   **3** Paste in order

1
2
3
4
5
6

Add bubble bath.

Get dressed.

Get out of the tub and dry off.

Get into the tub.

Fill the tub with water.

Wash with soap and a rag.

How to Make a Sandwich

1 Cut   **2** Read   **3** Paste in order

1
2
3
4
5
6

Cut the sandwich in two.

Open the jar of peanut butter.

Eat it up!

Get out the bread, peanut butter, and a knife.

Sit down and take a big bite.

Put a lot of peanut butter on the bread.

How to Plant a Seed

1 Cut   **2** Read   **3** Paste in order

1
2
3
4
5
6

Water the seeds.

Pick out the seeds you want to plant.

Fill the hole with dirt and pat it down.

Now the seeds can grow.

Next you must dig a hole in the dirt.

Drop the seeds into the hole.